Anthony Ivan

*A standalone story*
*of one of the 3,500 children*
*who are murdered by*
*their caregivers every year*

Jessica Jackson

*For the purposes of anonymity, names of
siblings and friends have been changed
unless where commonly known*

## *This book has details of child abuse
that some readers may find upsetting*

Every week in the UK
1-2 children are abused to death
by their parents or caregivers
In the USA, the number
is a staggering 27 children per week


*This is the story*
*of one of those children*


**This work is based on a real case**
*The first part of the story is semi-fictionalised,*
*with some events and dialogue added*

*The second part tells the facts of the case,*
*detailing the injuries, trials and sentencing*

# Contents

# Thank You For Choosing This Book

I wrote Anthony's story during the time between his murderers' convictions and their sentencing, and published on 25 April 2023, the day his mother and her (now ex) boyfriend were sentenced.

If you are reading this in early 2023, you may be familiar with the case. But as the months and years go by, I hope Anthony won't be forgotten.

I write to honour and remember him and all murdered children, in the hope of protecting children of the future.

> Reader reviews get my books noticed – perhaps that's what brought you here – so I'd be very grateful if you could spare a moment to **rate or review** this book when you've finished reading.

# Your Free Ebook

Exclusive only to my readers, and
not available in any bookstore:

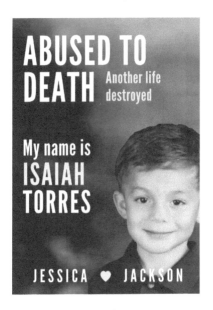

**The tragic case
of Isaiah Torres**

*(with bonus content about
Baby Brianna Lopez)*

**I'll let you know how to pick up your copy soon**

MY NAME IS ANTHONY AVALOS

8

# Introduction

On 20 June 2018, Heather Maxine Barron called 911 from her home in Lancaster, Los Angeles County.

Her son, Anthony Nolan Avalos, lay lifeless on the bedroom floor, covered from head to toe in bruises and abrasions.

First Responders who began chest compressions in an effort to revive him knew something wasn't right.

Instead of begging them to save her son's life, Barron repeatedly told the officers that she didn't hit her children, claiming, "I swear he was just acting up, and he threw himself because he didn't want to eat."

But the truth was quite different, and much more chilling.

# My Name is Anthony Avalos

And this is my story …

*(Dear Reader, please turn back a couple of pages for a short message from the author, and news of your FREE ebook)*

'You're quiet today, Anthony.'

'Oh, I'm okay.'

She brushes the hair off my forehead. 'You sure about that?'

I nod. I don't want her to know I've been crying.

'Don't you want to play in the pool with the others?'

'I guess.'

'Sitting here with your auntie, like you're 77 instead of just seven,' she teases. 'And look how much fun they're having.'

I watch them, giggling and squealing and splashing. But my little sister sits apart; quiet like me. Mommy was mean to her last night.

I spring up. 'Come on, sis. Let's jump in together.'

She takes my hand.

'One, two, three, go!'

'Well done, you guys,' calls Auntie Maria.

'I'm going to jump in by myself now,' says my little sister, scrambling out of the water.

'Okay, but maybe a bit less noise this time.' Our auntie nods to the baby in her stroller. 'This tiny one needs to sleep now.'

'Can I jump in? Please, Auntie?'

She smiles and shakes her head. 'What am I gonna do with you kids? Go on, then. Five more minutes of crazy-time, then we'll watch some TV before your Mommy comes to pick you up.'

I try to block out the words. Maybe she won't come, and we can stay here tonight.

'Come on, Anthony,' shouts my sister. 'Try and catch me.'

I hold out my arms, and she dive-bombs in. The water goes everywhere, and I look up at my auntie. But she's laughing as she reaches down to wipe the water from her legs.

I haul myself out of the pool. 'Can I rock the baby now?'

'Of course you can, Anthony. Just rub yourself a little drier first.'

I catch hold of the towel. 'I love it here, Auntie.'

'I know, my precious boy. I know.' She pats the lawn chair beside her. 'Come sit with me.'

I sit down and cuddle the baby.

'How's things at home?'

I shrug. 'Oh, you know.'

My auntie sighs. 'Mommy's not hurting you, is she?'

'Oh no. Mommy loves us.'

'I know. But we worry about you. Your mom has a bad temper.'

'I guess she does.' I snuggle in a bit closer. 'Ooh, I sometimes wish I could come and live with you.'

She touches my arm. 'Oh, Anthony.'

'With my brothers and sister.'

'Well, we couldn't leave them out, now could we?'

'Am I a good big brother?'

'You're kidding me. You're amazing.'

I've got a little sister and two little brothers, and we don't have the same dad. But that's okay.

'I love you, Auntie.'

'And I love you, my Anthony Nolan.'

(Nolan is my middle name, and only special people call me that.)

My little brothers and sister come panting out of the pool. 'Dry us, Anthony.'

'I can't, I've got the baby.'

'Here, I'll take her, sweetheart,' says my auntie. 'I have to go inside anyway and make something for you kids to eat. You're getting way too skinny for my liking.'

We give a big cheer.

'What would you like?'

'Pizza!'

Auntie laughs as she heads for the kitchen.

But then I remember. I turn to my brothers and sister. 'Mommy says we can't eat anything without permission.'

'We don't have to tell her, Anthony. Aren't you hungry?'

'Yeah, 'course I am. But I don't want us to get in trouble again.'

'But it's pizza, Anthony.'

'I know. I know. But Mommy said …'

'Well, I'm going to have some.'

I sigh and grab the towel and start to dry my youngest brother. 'I guess we *are* hungry, and if we don't tell …'

I was hoping she might be late, but Mommy comes early instead.

She grabs my brother's chin. 'What's that round your mouths? Is it tomato sauce?'

I lick my lips quickly.

'They just had a little leftover pizza, Heather,' says Auntie Maria.

'I've *told* you about feeding them.'

'It wasn't much. And after they used up all that energy in the pool, they were so hungry.'

Mommy scowls. 'So just whose kids are they? Who gets to say when they eat?'

I can sense Auntie trying to keep her temper. 'I know it's your job, Heather. But just this once I thought it'd be okay. And I had to feed my own kids anyway.'

'Not this once, not ever. You got that?' And she grabs my brothers' hands and drags them into the street.

I follow behind with my little sister.

'Hurry up,' she yells back at us. 'You're gonna get what's coming for eating food when I told you not to.'

'But it was Auntie,' says my brother. 'She said we were looking skinny.'

She drops their hands and grips his shoulders. 'I don't care what she says. Do you understand? You listen to what I say, and no one else. You got that?'

'Yes, Mommy.'

'It's too late. I'll be disciplining you when we get home.'

I hate that word: *discipline*. 'It was my fault, Mommy,' I say. 'I told them to eat the pizza.'

§

We all get beaten with the belt and sent to our rooms. But I can hear Mommy moving around.

I push open my bedroom door. 'Mommy?'

'Yeah, Anthony. What do you want?'

'Can I have a drink please?'

She shrugs. 'Just a sip.'

'I'm sorry we ate the pizza, Mommy.'

'It's okay. I shouldn't have gotten so mad at you.'

'I love you, Mommy.'

'Yeah, I guess you do.'

I'm sure she loves me too.

But I wish she would hug me.

Just once.

§

We're on the starting line. My feet are pinched in my shoes. But my heart is pounding with excitement.

'On your mark.'

We crouch to the ground.

'Get set.'

We've learnt to do it like the real athletes do, and we straighten our legs as we bend upwards.

'Go.'

I sprint as fast as I can, feeling strong and free, like I could do anything. I wish it would last forever. I'm grinning as I cross the line.

Anthony excelled at running & loved all sports

'You've done it again, Anthony,' says Mr Brown, patting me on the back.

'I love running,' I say. 'I'm going to try for the cup.'

'You have a very good chance, young man.' He turns to the two runners-up. 'You too, Marty, and you, Paul.'

'Have we, Sir?'

'For sure. But I'll need you all to practice after school.'

'We're the best runners in all California,' shouts Paul.

Mr Brown laughs. 'Not quite. Not yet, anyway. You're the best in the school for now. Maybe in the Valley. Anthony, are you okay?'

'I have chores after school.'

'We all have chores,' scoffs Marty. 'I have to mind my baby sister on Mondays and Thursdays.'

I look away, trying not to think of what happens in my house when school is over.

'Do you have chores every day?' asks Mr Brown.

I nod.

'We'll figure something out. Don't worry.'

'Thank you, Sir.'

'Right, off you go again, boys,' says Mr Brown. 'Might as well get some more practice right away.'

My auntie once told us that we could keep good feelings in a kind of memory box in our minds, so that we'll have nice things to think about when things aren't going too well. I put the feeling of sprinting to the finish line into my box.

§

I take my sister's hand as my uncle leads us out into the night. We're trying to be as quiet as mice, but with all my siblings and cousins, giggling and jumping up and down, it's not easy.

'Shh, kids,' whispers Uncle David. 'We want to surprise them.'

We creep up towards the door, a long line of excited kids. I'm chosen to knock at the first door. Then everyone else will take a turn.

'A bit louder, Anthony,' says my uncle.

A light comes on in the hallway.

'Trick or treat!'

The poor old lady looks terrified for a moment, before her face softens into a smile. 'Oh, you kids.'

My uncle starts to apologise for the crowd of monsters, pirates, and super-heroes on the lady's doorstep, but she's already reaching for a bag of goodies. 'These kids all yours?' the lady asks Uncle David.

I sometimes pretend that Uncle David is my dad and Auntie Maria is my mom.

Anthony loved Halloween and superheroes

Uncle David laughs and ruffles my sister's hair. 'Might as well be.'

We dance up and down the road, calling out to the other groups of kids knocking on doors across the street. My mouth is watering at the thought of the packs of Skittles and M&M's in my pumpkin bucket.

We shower my auntie Crystal with our treats when we get back. She's Uncle David's sister, which means she's

Mommy's sister too, and we always get extra hugs when she visits from out of town.

'So these are all for me then?' she laughs, snatching up a couple of bags of candy corn.

We all yell, 'No!' as loud as we can, reaching up to grab them as she dangles them above our heads. When one of my little cousins starts to get upset, she swoops them down onto the table and we sort out all the packets again into what belongs to each of us.

'Everyone out back,' calls Uncle David. 'The hot dogs are ready.' And we rush out towards the smell of sausages sizzling on the grill. We know better than to fool around near the hot stove, so we get in line until we're handed a hot dog and then go sit on the grass, licking our lips.

When the music starts playing we pick up our glow-sticks and jump up and dance around like crazy for hours.

'Who wants a candy apple?' says Auntie Maria, and we clamber over each other to be the first to get one of our favourite treats.

I add this night to the memory box.

§

'Let's have a quiet day, today,' I say to Auntie Maria the next morning when the other kids are still in bed.

'Oh, wouldn't that be nice,' she smiles. 'You tired, my little man?'

'Only a bit.' I pass her the milk carton. 'But I just feel, I don't know, quiet.'

I always feel like this when we've had a great time at my auntie and uncle's house, and I know we have to go back home.

Auntie Maria knows what I'm thinking. 'She's not coming till this evening.'

'So we've got the whole day?'

'Yes, Anthony. The whole day.'

That heavy feeling slides off my shoulders.

Auntie hugs me. 'Want to do some crafts this morning?'

'I'd love that.' I like making things, cutting out shapes, sticking them down to make a nice picture, helping the little ones. 'Maybe I'll manage to make something Mom will like.'

Anthony was creative and enjoyed arts and crafts

Auntie Maria sighs. 'Yeah, maybe.'

'I'll make her a card. I'll tell her how much I love her.'

'Oh, Anthony.'

'She loves me, Auntie.'

'I guess so, sweetheart.'

'She really does.'

'I know, I know.'

Uncle David comes into the kitchen with the baby in his arms, and three of my cousins following behind.

'We're all starving.' He twirls my auntie round the room with his free hand. 'What's for breakfast?'

§

Mommy's new boyfriend is called Kareem Leiva.

He's not supposed to live with us, because we're in low-income housing, and with Kareem earning a lot of money at work, it takes our family above the limit. But he's here all the time, so I think he does live with us. It's another one of the times that Mommy tells us: "What happens in the house, stays in the house." Like being hit with the cable of the vacuum or locked in our rooms.

Kareem is very big and very mean. And just like with Mommy, when he says "jump," we ask "how high?" He's got kids of his own, and they're quite nice to us. But Kareem isn't nice to us. Not nice at all.

§

'For being kind and caring, this month's gold star goes to Anthony Avalos.'

'He always gets it,' mumbles one of my class-mates. 'And he hasn't been here as long as the rest of us.'

He's right. I used to go to Lincoln Elementary but Mommy took me out of there when I got the two black eyes, and Vice-Principal Greaux called welfare on her.

'Thank you, Miss.'

'And today we have a new class member. His name is Michael, and his family has just moved here from upstate New York.'

'Wow, that's way over on the east coast,' says Lisa.

'That's right. Now, children, I want you all to give Michael a nice welcome and help him out, okay?'

I raise my hand. 'There's a spare seat beside me, Miss.'

'Thank you, Anthony. Michael, go and sit by Anthony, and he'll show you how we do things here.'

Michael shuffles into he seat beside me, and grins. I grin back. We don't have many blond kids in my school.

'Let's have a little geography lesson,' says Mrs Bell. 'Who can tell me how far away New York is from here in LA?'

§

'Why don't you spank your kids real hard, Auntie?' I'm in the kitchen, helping her making tamales.

'Well, I guess I don't want to hurt them, Anthony.'

'You don't?'

'No, I just want to let them know they did wrong. But I can do that with a little tap and then talking to them.'

'Oh, okay. That sounds pretty good.'

'And they're only really naughty once in a while. So I don't need to do it much.'

'You sure can shout sometimes though.'

Auntie Maria laughs. 'I guess so. Anyway, why did you ask me about spanking them hard, mijo?'

'Oh, it's nothing.'

She takes a breath. 'Does Mommy spank you guys hard, Anthony?'

I think of the beating my brother got last night after he moved when Mom had us all kneel on rice for two hours. Then she made him do the Captain's Chair. 'Sometimes.'

'She does? I thought she stopped all that after Children's Services came by last time.'

'She did. For a while.'

'Oh, baby. Is it the same? Locking you in your room?'

'Yeah, stuff like that. We get so thirsty, Auntie Maria.'

She sighs. 'We'll call them again, Anthony.'

'They never talk to us kids. They only talk to Mommy.'

'Uncle David will tell them to talk to you.'

'Without Mom?'

'Definitely without Mom.'

The other kids are calling me from the back yard.

'Anything else you want to tell me, my Anthony Nolan?'

I shrug. 'That's about it. But I

Ready for a game of football or basketball

23

can tell you anything, can't I?'

'Sure, you can.'

So I run outside and join the game of basketball.

§

My cousins and my class-mates will be finishing their breakfasts round about now, and getting ready for school.

On the other side of my bedroom door, I hear my sister begging to go too. I know Mommy will say "no", because of her face. My sister's really pretty, but she was bleeding so bad, and I guess the latest bruises will be coming up.

'No, you aren't going,' shouts Mommy.

Just as I expected. None of us will be allowed to go today.

My sister has been crying all night after Kareem beat her in the face with the ping-pong bat. He said she'd moved when we'd been told to stand still in the corner. She'd shivered. That's all.

I hate to hear my sister crying.

Last night was a bad one. My eyes and throat are still stinging from the hot sauce, and I couldn't sleep for the pain everywhere.

School gets us away from them for a while, and we might get a hug from one of our teachers. And I don't want to miss my lessons. I love writing stories, but sometimes

I'm so tired I can't even think of easy words and how to spell them. I'm not the best runner in my class anymore either.

Pretty soon, I hear kids skipping down the street, laughing at each others' jokes, then minding their mothers as they tell them to look out for cars when they cross the road.

I try to think up my own joke.

Knock, knock.

*Who's there?*

Woody.

*Woody who?*

Woody be okay if I told someone about Mommy and Kareem again?


The front door slams as Mommy sets off for work.

'Anthony.' My sister's voice is faint.

'I'm here.'

'Can you open the door?'

'I can't. I'm locked in too.'

'I was going to tell the teacher today.'

'Maybe tomorrow.'

But I know she'll be too scared to tell. So will I.


The day drags on. I've mostly been sleeping. My tummy has stopped growling, but the thirst is still unbearable. I had to go to the bathroom in my shorts. Twice.

Before Kareem came, I would look forward to getting out of my room again, but now we don't know if we'll get more punishments when the door gets unlocked. I ask Jesus if we'll be allowed a drink of water.

I wish I had a pencil and some paper to write on. I'd like to write to my aunties and my teachers.

§

'Whoa there, Anthony,' says Uncle David.

I pull on the rod as hard as I can.

'Looks like supper's on you tonight, fella.'

'I can't hold it.'

'Sure, you can,' he says, and puts his arms over mine as we draw the fish out of the water together.

Uncle David laughs. 'Well, maybe it'll feed the baby and a couple of the other little ones.'

I try not to feel too disappointed as the small fish plops onto the ground.

'We'll tell them you caught a whopper but we threw it back in.'

'Yes, because it wanted to go back to its friends.'

Fishing with Uncle David & his siblings & cousins

'I don't mind fibbing if you don't.'

26

Uncle David always has a way of making me smile. I hug him.

'Hang on there, little buddy.'

'What's up?'

'I could see you were getting a little skinny, Anthony, but there's hardly anything left of you.'

'Oh, I'm alright.'

Uncle David starts to unpack our picnic. I spot my favourite sandwiches. 'Tell me what's going on, son.'

I sit beside him on the grass. 'Nothing. Nothing's going on.'

'You were talking to your auntie Maria. She said you started to tell her stuff. Anthony, you don't have to be scared to tell me.'

'But they'll beat us if we say things.'

'You trust me, don't you, son?'

I swallow hard and nod. Uncle David is so kind, and it makes me miss my real Daddy.

He puts his arm around my shoulders.

'Hey, Champ. Hey, you don't have to cry.'

I'm wetting my uncle's shirt. 'I'm just a cry-baby.'

'No. No, you're not. You're upset and I want to know about it. Okay?'

I take a deep breath. 'We're getting beat on, Uncle David. And we don't get enough to eat. Or to drink; that's the worst. And I can't take care of my brothers and sister.'

'You're such a good kid.' He squeezes my shoulder. 'Is it your mom, or Kareem?'

'Both.'

'Are you getting locked in your room again?'

I nod. I tell him about having to kneel on uncooked rice until our knees bleed.

'Anthony, I don't want you going back there, okay?'

I want to believe it, but I'm scared to. 'Do you think they'll let us stay with you this time?'

'They'd damned well better do. No mother should be doing this to her kids.'

'Kareem is so big and strong, Uncle David.'

'He won't hurt me, Anthony. It's just little kids he picks on.'

I'm not sure why I'm crying so much. And when Uncle David takes me into his arms for a bear hug, I cry even more. 'I'm scared to go back there, Uncle David.'

'Maria, we're keeping them here.'

'Oh, thank God,' says my auntie, wiping her baby's face. 'It just can't carry on like this.' She smiles at me. 'So, we've got to put up with you, Anthony Nolan Avalos!'

I laugh as she holds out her arms to me. 'I'll be able to call you "Mommy" now, won't I?'

She hesitates.

'Could I? I mean if we do get to stay here?'

'Yes, my little man, that'd be nice.'

'So, what can we have to eat?' Uncle David winks at my auntie. 'Us fishermen are hungry.'

'But, Uncle David, we just …'

He puts his finger to his lips. 'Hungry work, this fishing.'

Auntie Maria turns to the fridge. 'Who you going to tell, David? About the kids?'

'Y'know, this time, I might not say anything. We just won't send them home.'

'Peanut butter and jelly okay, Anthony?'

'Yes, please, Auntie Maria. Did my brothers and sister eat already?'

'You think I don't know how to feed you hungry kids?'

We're both laughing.

'That's one thing I do know, Anthony Nolan.'

'You sure do, Auntie.'

'Good. Now get that sandwich eaten up. It'll soon be time for dinner.'

§

Auntie Maria jumps at the knock on the door. 'Is it Leiva?'

'I don't think so, honey.'

Uncle David opens the door to his sister, my mom.

'I've been waiting.' She starts to walk inside. 'How come you never brought the kids back?'

Uncle David bars Mom's way. 'You're not having them back. Not this time.'

Auntie gathers my siblings and me to her. 'Don't worry, kids. This time it'll get sorted.'

I can see Mom through the doorway, doing one of her 'Who-do-think-you're-talking-to?' faces. I move out of sight.

'I'm not having my kids back? Are you for real?'

'You're hurting them again, Heather. You can't keep doing that.'

'I can do whatever the fuck I want, brother.'

'No. Not anymore. Not with the kids. Use your head, Heather. You're doing what Mom and Dad did to us. You can stop it. Like Crystal and me did. You have to stop it.'

'I don't have to listen to this horseshit. Send my kids out right now.'

Uncle David lowers his voice. 'No, Heather.'

'What've they been saying?'

'They don't need to say anything. They're bruised, and they're scared.'

'I'll give them scared. Now send them out, I'm warning you.'

'You're locking them in their rooms again. Not giving them enough to eat or drink.'

Mommy laughs. 'David, you dummy. You know what kids are like. They'll say anything to get what they want. You been spoiling them? Like you spoil your own lot?'

Auntie starts to get up out of the chair, but my uncle waves his arm for her to sit down again.

'They've been hungry, Heather. Let us look after them till we get this straightened out.'

'Straightened out? You just want to take my own kids off of me.'

'You need to get some help, sis. Then you could take them back.'

'Wait till Kareem hears about this. He'll go crazy. You don't mess with that guy, David. You should know that.'

'About Kareem,' says my uncle. 'He's beating the kids, isn't he? Making them stand in a corner for hours.'

Mom shakes her head. 'You'll be sorry, David. I mean it. You'll be real sorry.'

§

An hour later, someone else comes to the door.

'Mr David Barron?'

'Yes, Sir. Come right in.'

The police officer takes a seat at the table. 'Might be better without the kids present. I've had a call from Heather Barron. Says you won't return her kids.'

'I'd like the kids to stay, if that's okay. They know pretty much everything. And I want Anthony to tell you what's been going on.'

'I understand, Sir. But let's have the kids out of the way for now, and I promise I'll speak to Heather's children in a little while. That okay?'

'Sure, that's fine, Officer …'

'Gelardo.' He shakes my uncle's hand.

'Anthony,' says Auntie Maria. 'Go take the kids to play upstairs.'

I try to hear through the bedroom door, but my cousins are giggling and dragging me into their game. When I see my brothers and sister laughing, I try and try to think of how I can stop Mommy and Kareem from hurting them so bad. I hope we don't get sent back tonight. Or any night.

It's not long before Auntie Maria calls for me. 'There's nothing to worry about, Anthony. He's a real nice man.'

She's right. Officer Gelardo speaks gently to me, and when he nods, I feel he believes me. I don't tell him everything, but I do tell about being locked inside and beaten.

The deputy turns to my auntie and uncle. 'I have to say that I don't feel these kids should be going home right now. You okay to ring Children's Services?'

Uncle David shrugs. 'We've called them so many times.'

'Okay. I'll ring the hotline and report my findings.'


I don't know what happened, but a couple days later, we have to go back to Mom's house.

I don't get to go fishing with Uncle David in Apollo Park anymore. Ever.

I just have to keep taking our last trip out of my memory box and think of his arms around me as he helped me catch that little fish.

Why doesn't telling ever help us?

§

'Get in here, Anthony. The both of you, get in here.'

I hold my little brother's hand. We don't have a choice; when Kareem calls us, we have to go.

I stand in front of my brother. 'He didn't do anything.'

'Liar. Your mother saw you.'

I look at Mom.

'You drank from the bathroom tap.'

'It wasn't him,' I say. 'It was just me, I promise.'

'I saw you,' says Mommy. 'Both of you.'

I know better than to say any more.

'Captain's Chair,' says Kareem quietly.

My brother and I stand side by side, our backs against the wall.

'Slide down.'

We bend our knees, our backs still touching the wall.

'Keep going.'

'Honey, I don't think they can go any lower.'

'I'll say when they can stop.'

My calves and thighs are burning already, and my little brother starts to whimper.

'Okay, low enough.'

With nothing to eat for the last two days, I know my brother feels as weak as I do. We won't be able to stay in position. But somehow we have to. We just have to, because even though we don't know what else is coming, we know it'll be something worse.

'Come in here and watch,' calls Mom to our sister.

Her face is already streaked with tears.

I pray to Jesus that they won't make her do the Captain's Chair too. He listens to that prayer.

My brother is crying and trembling. His legs won't hold him, and if he falls, Kareem will beat him. The last time he beat me, I was unconscious for what seemed like forever. My brother won't be able to stand that. I fall to the floor.

'Lazy piece of shit,' roars Kareem, as he kicks my back.

I scream in agony.

'Oh, shut up, Anthony, you faggot,' says Mom. 'It doesn't hurt.'

Kareem kicks my brother's legs from under him and he topples to the floor beside me.

Mom and Kareem are laughing fit to burst. 'Look at the two of them. Can't stand up for five minutes.'

'Absolutely useless,' says Mom.

Tears are stinging my eyes. Why does Mommy think we're useless? We'd do anything to make her proud of us, but nothing works.

Kareem kicks my brother in the stomach. Then he grabs my ear and drags me up. 'How did you manage to give birth to this faggot?' He turns to my brother. 'You, up.'

My brother holds onto me for balance. I try to whisper that it'll be okay.

'Now, fight.'

We stare at Kareem.

'You heard me. Fight each other. Come on, I want to see blood.'

I turn to Mom. 'Please, Mom. We can't fight each other.'

She folds her arms. 'You heard your stepfather.'

I'm frantically trying to think what to do. 'I can't hurt him. I can't. Mom, please.'

'Get on with it. And do it for real. No pretending.'

*Please Jesus. Make them change their minds. I can't fight my brother.*

'What a pair of wimps,' yells Kareem. 'Get fighting. And the loser gets a whupping, so fight hard and try to win.'

With my arm still supporting my brother, I throw a gentle punch at his chest.

'I. Told. You. To. Fight. Do it. Or I'll fight each of you in turn. So, fight. Now.'

35

Somehow, I pretend to lose without Kareem noticing. But he still beats us both anyway.

All night, I can hear the sound of my little brother crying. I know how he feels because I feel the same. Terrified and in pain. I didn't protect him.

My other little brother got taken away by his daddy, so I don't have to worry about him. I'm glad he got away. But I miss his cheeky smile. I wonder what he's doing now.

I need the memory box real bad, and in my mind, I'm staying with Mommy's sister, Auntie Crystal, who lives far away. I remember one visit when she had something special planned for us to do every day. Auntie Crystal gives amazing cuddles too, and if I concentrate real hard, I can imagine she's squeezing me tight.

My brother and me are kept off school all week. And we still hardly get anything to eat or drink.

§

'What you got there, Anthony?'

I grip my bible tighter. 'Please don't take it, Mrs Bell.'

'I won't, honey. Why would I want to go and do that?'

'I don't know. But I like to keep it close to me.'

'That's okay, Anthony. It's a good thing to have your bible around. God is taking care of you.'

'Do you really think he is, Miss?'

'Sure I do. Don't you, sweetheart?'

'I guess.'

'You going to stand here talking or you going to help me collect up these papers?'

'I'm going to help you, Miss!'

'You take this side and I'll take the other. Okay?'

I don't want to be apart from my teacher, even though she's just on the other side of the room, so I pick up my papers quickly and go across to her.

'Slow down! You're making me look bad.'

I grin. Mrs Bell's a real good friend to me. I'll miss her during summer break, but she's my teacher again in fifth grade so I'll see her all next year. I reach out to help her with a couple of books and drop my bible. I freeze. Then I start to cry.

'Hey, hey, Anthony. It's okay.' She hands it to me. 'What's upsetting you, hon?'

Anthony was a bright and hardworking pupil

'I don't like to drop my bible.'

'I know, Anthony. But it's okay. Look, you get ahold of it nice and tight again.'

I try not to let her see me kiss it before I put it under my arm. 'I'll miss you in the holidays.'

'And I'll miss you.'

'You will?'

'Of course I will. And who's going to draw those lovely pictures for my girls?'

'If I came to your house I could do some more drawings.'

She crouches down in front of me and strokes my hair.

I put it in the memory box.

'Oh, Anthony. Maybe one day when you're older. But you know I live a way out of town. And your mommy doesn't like you to go far from home.'

I nod. 'Maybe I'll see you at the store.'

'Maybe. If I'm in town.'

'But we'll always see each other, won't we? Even when I go up to Middle School.'

'I hope so. Feeling better now?'

'A bit.'

'Good boy. Hey, Anthony, you've been really kind to Michael.'

'I remember what it's like to feel new. And lonely.'

'Well, good job. You've helped him settle in real well.'

'Thank you, Miss.' I reach into my pocket with my free hand. 'Well, I guess it's time to go. Have a great summer, Mrs Bell.' I hand her the note I spent all week writing. 'Just so you won't miss me too much.'

'Thank you, Anthony. Bye now.'

'Bye, Miss. I'm already looking forward to August.'

§

'Remember I told you about the new boy at school, Mom?'

Mom isn't usually interested in things I tell her, but maybe today. Since I'm not allowed to see my auntie and uncle anymore, I miss the chance to talk about school and stuff.

'Uh-uh?'

'Yes, his name's Michael. He's a good runner, just like me.'

'Oh, you're good at something then, are you?'

'You know I'm good at running, Mom.'

'Yeah, whatever.'

'And I really like Michael, Mom.'

'Oh yeah?'

She's half-listening. At least that's something.

'Yes, I like boys *and* girls, Mom. Some of the boys are real nice.'

'What did you say?'

'That there's a new boy in school. And I like him.'

'What's the little faggot saying?' I didn't realise Kareem was in the next room.

'He's saying he likes boys,' says Mom.

'I like boys *and* girls, Mommy. Both the same.'

I don't see the punch to my head coming.

'Filthy faggot!' yells Kareem. 'Can't stand them anywhere near me.'

Mom has 'the look'. She changes into the Devil and I get so scared. I hope they'll just lock me in my room again. But they don't.

I wonder what Auntie Maria and Uncle David are doing now. And if I could sneak out and get to their house on my own.

§

I can just about make out their voices above the noises and weird feelings in my head.

'We need to lay off. We won't be able to send him to school like that.'

'They haven't bothered much before.'

'Are you crazy? They've been here a thousand times.'

'Yeah, but they never really do anything.'

'I suppose. And there's still plenty of time left.'

'Good, because he sure hasn't been punished enough for being a dirty fucking faggot.'

Kareem yells the last bit into my face.

Someone shouts. 'Mommy, Mommy. Stop him.'

A slap.

'But he wasn't having a temper tantrum. He'll be good, Mommy.'

Another voice. A little girl crying.

*Don't cry, mija. I'll be okay.*

I try to say their names. But I can't remember what they are. I can see their faces though; giggling when we went trick or treating that last time. I think I mumble something, and Kareem's laughter comes out of somewhere above me.

'Little bastard's trying to speak.' He punches my face. 'Don't you dare speak. Get the hot sauce; that'll shut him up.'

I splutter and try to beg them to stop pouring the sauce into my mouth. My whole face is on fire as it gushes out of the bottle and all over me.

'Kareem. Maybe we should stop now.'

'Don't you tell me what to do.'

*Dear Jesus, please tell them to leave me alone.*

'He needs a few more bounces.'

*Please don't pick me up again.*

But I feel myself being lifted by my ankles and my head points to the ground again. He's so tall that he can hold me above the floor before crashing me down head-first.

My throat is too raw to scream.

'I'll knock the fucking faggot out of him.'

*No, no. Where's my bible? If I had my bible I could really pray to you, Jesus.*

I know I'm going to die. Everything keeps going black and then each time they swing me up I jolt awake, screaming.

'You're going to kill him, Kareem.'

'Don't be stupid. You think he can't handle a few knocks to the head.'

'I don't know. What if he can't?'

I'm thrown against the wall, and I slide to the floor.

'Don't you touch him.' That's Kareem again. 'He hasn't learnt his lesson yet.'

'Maybe just a sip of water, honey.'

'No. Leave him, Heather. I'm warning you.'

It all goes quiet again. I think I'm alone in my room. Somebody rattles the handle but I guess the door is locked.

'Anthony.' It's my sister. 'We're going to tell, Anthony.'

'Can you hear us?' says my brother.

'Get away from that door,' yells Mommy. And I hear the belt whipping through the air.

After that, all the sounds are muffled.

§

I crawl towards the window. But when I get there, it's not a window at all; it's my Batman poster. I slump against the wall, and my body starts to shake. Water dribbles out of my ears and nose, and I vomit down my chest.

I whisper: 'Mommy, help me.' But I'm not thinking of Mommy at all. I'm thinking of Auntie Maria and Uncle David and all my cousins. I'm thinking of Auntie Crystal and her family. I'm thinking of my brothers and sisters. I'm thinking of my daddy, and all his side of the family. I'm thinking of my grandparents. I'm thinking of Mrs Bell and all my teachers. I'm thinking of everyone who loves me. Everyone who would help me if they could.

The pain in my head is unbearable. It feels like my brain is trying to push its way out of my skull. I need something good to cling to, so in my mind, I take out my memory box.

I remember that day I won a prize at school and my whole family came. On my dad's side too. And I spoke to Daddy that night to tell him all about it.

I keep the memory box with me as Mommy and Kareem unlock the door and come into the room and start it all again.

I know I'm going to die this time. But I feel like everyone is with me, and I won't be afraid. Not anymore.

I hope someone will take care of my little brother and sister.

**My name is Anthony Avalos**

**And I was abused to death**

**Thank you for reading my story**

**Please don't forget me**

It's time to hand over to Jessica again, who now tells a more factual **account of my life and death** …

# The Murder of Anthony Avalos

Anthony Nolan Avalos
04.05.08 – 21.06.18
aged 10 years & 1 month
LA County, California

On 20 June 2018, Heather Barron called 911 from her home in the 1100 block of East Avenue K, Lancaster, LA County.

First Responders who arrived at the scene late that night described a little boy, covered from head to toe in bruises and abrasions, and with circular burn marks on his stomach, lying unresponsive, without a pulse.

Deputy David Pine was the first to arrive, and although he felt that Anthony appeared to be dead already, he started chest compressions in an effort to revive him.

The deputies knew instantly that something wasn't right. The mother's explanation that the little boy had thrown himself back during a tantrum, hitting his head, before falling to his bedroom floor, did not ring true. Deputy Adan Ordaz found Heather Barron's overall behaviour strange. She "didn't seem really distressed." Her son lay lifeless on the floor, and she wasn't crying or hysterical.

Instead, she was at great pains to tell the deputy that she didn't hit her children, and she asked if she was going to be taken to jail.

When two of Heather Barron's other children were being spoken to in an upstairs room, her focus was not on her dead or dying son. Instead, she was desperate to know why they were questioning her other kids. "I didn't do anything," she repeatedly claimed.

Another red flag were the almost identical words used by Anthony's siblings: "My mom doesn't hit me, nobody hits us." The deputy who was questioning them also felt that some of the words used by the seven- and eight-year-olds, such as 'discipline' and 'temper tantrums' were suspicious.

"Everybody is telling me I'm a bad mom," Heather Barron wails, when taken in for questioning by detectives. "They keep on looking at me like ... if I hurt him, and I, and I didn't. I swear he was just acting up, and he threw himself because he didn't want to eat. He didn't want to eat. That's it."

When subsequently asked about the scrapes and bruises on her son's knees, Barron attributed them to playing basketball and attested that what looked like cigarette burns were probably spider bites.

However, it later transpired that Anthony had been systematically tortured for two weeks straight, with hot sauce poured onto his face and body, being beaten and whipped, thrown into furniture, smacked in the face with a ping-pong paddle, and hung or held upside down, and repeatedly dropped on his head; the act that finally killed him.

While her son lay dying on the floor, his mother had waited a whole day or more before calling the police, concocting with her boyfriend an 'explanation' for Anthony's death. Then Kareem Leiva fled the home with two of his own children.

Anthony, about whom the medical staff said, "was so malnourished and dehydrated that his veins were collapsed" was pronounced dead in hospital the following day. Amid growing suspicions about the ten-year-old's death, seven other children from the home were taken into protective custody.

§

Anthony was born to Heather Barron and Victor Avalos on May 4, 2008 in Los Angeles County, California, US, when the pair were still in their teens. Victor Avalos left the area soon after his son was born, moving to Mexico to find work, after which he didn't see his son again, speaking to him on occasional video calls. During Barron's trial, Victor Avalos testified that she had rebuffed his attempts to see his child.

Innocent and trusting

Anthony was the only child the couple had between them.

I apologise if this next paragraph is confusing, regarding the children of Heather Barron and Kareem Leiva.

Following Anthony's birth, Barron went on to have a further six children with other men; three of whom were with Leiva. Leiva had eight children, including the three with Barron. Not all Leiva's children lived with him, but all Heather's did, until one birth father removed his son to safety, around seven months before Anthony's death. I believe there were ten children in the home at the time of the murder, with two then fleeing with Leiva, their father, and seven being removed when their mother was taken into custody.

Although Anthony had only half-siblings, out of respect to their closeness and shared experiences in the home, I have chosen not to use the prefix "half".

Heather Barron lived off welfare and a part-time job at Subway.

§

The children's troubles, and involvement with child protection services, began early in their lives.

Taking Anthony to a clinic when he was just four years old, his mother reported that he had been sexually abused by his step-grandfather. The Department for Children and

Family Services (DCFS) confirmed that the abuse had taken place, but after Barron reassured them that she would arrange support for her son and protect him from his abuser, the department withdrew from the case.

Heather Barron did not set up the promised counselling.

At the age of five, Anthony began his schooling at Lincoln Elementary, where Vice-Principal Gia Greaux quickly became concerned for his welfare, after he disclosed a variety of punishments, including denial of food, water and use of the bathroom. He also told the educator that he was forced to squat with his back against the

Anthony diligently learning how to write his name.

wall, with his arms outstretched. This recognised form of torture, known as 'The Captain's Chair' is valuable to the perpetrator, as it leaves no physical evidence. Vice-Principal Greaux called the child abuse hotline on at least one occasion.

At six years old, Anthony confided in his aunt Crystal (Heather Barron's sister) that his mom beat him and locked him in a room. As a result, the child abuse hotline was called, and a caseworker spoke to Anthony at school. Though Anthony and his siblings were being neglected, and were deemed 'high risk', instead of intervention appropriate to this risk level, the family was referred to the department's Voluntary Family Maintenance program, with counselling provided for the family by the Children's Centre of the Antelope Valley. Whilst this may sound promising on the surface, the program was set up for lower risk children, where it is felt that they are safe to remain in the home, and where caregivers are highly motivated to work on the issues that caused the abuse, with a view to preventing its recurrence.

Making this decision not to allocate appropriate services for high risk children, were Mark Millman and Matthew Mansfield, the latter being one of the case workers who had also contributed to Gabriel Fernandez' injudicious placement in the voluntary program.

(Please see my book: '*My Name is Gabriel Fernandez*' for Gabriel's story.)

Thus began a litany of missed opportunities to protect the children.

Counsellors at the centre received little or no support from the DCFS caseworkers, despite their grave concerns about Barron: "her capacity to provide suitable care for her children is severely limited by her poor parenting skills, poor judgment and denial and lack of awareness of her mental health issues," counsellor Luis Ramirez wrote in June 2014.

Another counsellor, Wendy Wright, called the child abuse hotline in October to report Barron's violent behaviour, and her habit of talking about her children in derogatory terms, saying that she displayed "nothing but anger toward those children."

Wright also felt that Mark Millman was lacking interest in the case, and did not seem to act on the counsellors' concerns. Despite being aware that Barron "cursed, yelled and acknowledged hitting the children with a belt", Millman stated that: "given the children and their age and their behaviour, *she is doing all she can*."

In November 2014, a third therapist, Crystal Gee, also called the child abuse hotline to report that one of the children had told her: "Mommy whoops our asses."

Again, her concerns were not adequately followed up.

At the end of 2014, to the shock and consternation of the counsellors who had been working with the family, Millman and Mansfield replaced the services of the Children's Centre with those of Hathaway-Sycamores Child and Family Services.

This new agency employed Barbara Dixon (one of those who, in 2017, would be questioned in the criminal case against the caseworkers who neglected to help Gabriel Fernandez prior to his death in 2013). Dixon admitted that she witnessed extensive injuries, but did not report to the child abuse hotline, in violation of the duties of her professional role.

Heart-breakingly, Dixon's counselling notes, which span an 11-month-period, reveal that she felt Anthony was prone to "whining," "crying" and "tantrums" and she advised him to "listen to his mother more attentively and to finish his homework". She failed to include notes of new allegations of abuse that were reported to the child abuse hotline during this time.

(In April 2022, Dixon faced charges of gross negligence and unprofessional conduct, in a disciplinary hearing, and was ordered to serve four years probation by The Board of Behavioural Sciences, requiring her to undergo training in psychotherapy, law and ethics and child abuse assessment.)

Following the arrests of Barron and Leiva after Anthony's murder, the DCFS did not comment on whether any employees had been disciplined, and a spokesperson told Newsweek: "DCFS takes a continuous quality improvement approach to evaluate policies and practices that may be enhanced to strengthen our system and, similarly, assess the need for corrective actions with individual employees."

They said that a number of changes had been brought into force, with thousands more social workers being taken on, in order to reduce caseloads.

§

We can clearly see that Anthony and his siblings were already enduring abuse prior to Heather Barron meeting Kareem Leiva in 2015, when Anthony was seven.

Leiva, who was an El Salvador native, had fathered five children, three of whom came to live with him and Barron. She had custody of her four children, before having three kids with Leiva. Whilst both 'caregivers' were allegedly abusive to all the children, Leiva was particularly so to his non-biological children.

According to court documents, Leiva's violence was not reserved only for children. In 2010 and 2013, he had been accused of domestic violence against his partners, and whilst in jail, it is said that he shanked (which means to stab with a makeshift blade, such as a piece of glass) another inmate.

In addition, both Barron and Leiva were known to be violently homophobic, and tragically, a ten-year-old boy saying that he liked boys as well as girls was deemed sufficient reason to be viciously abused for two weeks straight. In the supposedly enlightened times in which we live, we have come to expect less rage against gay people. But it is often a perpetrator's doubts and fears about their own sexuality that triggers such a massive over-reaction.

§

Whilst there are surely many instances of appropriate steps being taken by the police and children's services to protect children, my research repeatedly leads me to discover numerous instances of inadequacies and incompetence. Anthony's case is no exception.

As mentioned, failings by social workers are often highlighted in cases of child murder by abuse. But law enforcement officers are frequently just as negligent.

When, in 2015, the father of one of Anthony's siblings alleged the abuse of his son by Leiva, DCFS duly alerted the police. But Deputy Chris Wyatt made no attempt to find Leiva, nor investigate the claim.

However, DCFS were obliged to follow it through, and when also assigned to the case, Deputy Billy Cox, who had been disciplined in the past for failing to properly investigate an unrelated child abuse allegation, did not contact Barron or Leiva.

Cox's court testimony is alarming: "It was routine and common practice," he said, "that if a referral was called in by a social worker, that we basically rubber-stamped it, so to speak, and sent it through."

I believe that the little boy's father was ultimately successful in removing him from the Barron-Leiva home and into his own care and protection.

§

In 2016, a worker at the daycare attended by Anthony's younger siblings also called the helpline, when she noticed bruising on their faces. She reported that the children had told her that their mom wouldn't allow them to eat, and that one of them had had to dig through the trash to find food.

It was further claimed that Anthony and his siblings were also burned with a curling iron, punished with wrestling moves, and forced to fight each other, with the loser facing even more brutal treatment.

Around this time, no doubt alarmed that her abuse was attracting attention from his teachers, Barron moved Anthony from Lincoln to a different school, El Dorado Elementary, away from those who had suspicions about her treatment of the children.

§

Anthony loved, and was loved by, his teachers at his new school. He was a bright pupil who excelled in class, and was caring towards his class-mates, helping his teacher by picking up things from the floor and passing out papers.

If you have any doubt as to the kind, respectful young man Anthony would have grown up to be, here's the letter he wrote to his teacher as he finished 4th grade at El Dorado. Harmony Bell would also have been his teacher had Anthony had the chance to move up to 5th grade, after which, in 6th grade, he would have moved up to New Vista Middle School.

Side note: by this time, Heather Barron had already cut off ties with loving members of Anthony's family, who had reported her actions, and we see how he longed to be in the company of adults he felt safe and secure with, as he had previously felt with caring aunts and uncles. This helps to explain why Anthony didn't confide in his beloved teacher, as he knew his mother might prevent him from seeing her again.

I cannot read his words without tears for this precious boy.

Anthony's heart-breaking
letter to his teacher,
Harmony Bell

He writes:

Dear Mrs Bell

Thank you for teaching me everything you could. It was such a blessing to meet you. I just hope that when I'm going up to the 6th that you can come to New Vista so I can see you still. I hope that you can come to my high school, middle school, college. That way we will see each other for school years without a problem, because how close we are and how we are best buddies/friends. I just wish I can come to your house sometimes because how much I miss you over the weekends and summer breaks. I just hope we can see each other every single year from 2018 and until you die.

… So I hope you have a great life if you can't see me every single year.

… I just want to stay with you forever but I can't. I just hope you have a good rest of your life because you already know that I'm going to have a good life. So I'm hoping you will too. Thank you for teaching me in 4th grade.

Love, Anthony Avalos, your friend.

MY NAME IS ANTHONY AVALOS

With the long summer vacation stretching ahead, Anthony would have known he had to endure at least eight weeks of his mother and stepfather's abuse.

But after graduating the fourth grade on 7 June 2018, Anthony was tortured every day until his death two weeks later.

§

Many parallels have been drawn between Gabriel Fernandez and Anthony, partly due to the references made about Anthony (and another LA County boy, Noah Cuatro), towards the end of the Netflix documentary, *The Trials of Gabriel Fernandez*.

Their homes were just a 15-minute drive apart in the Antelope Valley, in Los Angeles County. They were 'served' by the same Department of Child and Family Services, they were both ridiculed for being gay before being tortured and murdered by their mother and boyfriend. Gabriel was eight years old and died in 2013, while Anthony was just turned ten when he died in 2018. Perhaps their paths had crossed as little boys visiting the shopping mall or playing with friends and cousins on the streets of Palmdale or Lancaster.

When I write the stories of the children, the families who loved them are never far from my thoughts. Like those who knew and loved Gabriel Fernandez, Anthony Avalos had a large and loving family. They never asked to be thrust into the spotlight, but now they work tirelessly to keep his memory alive, and to prevent the suffering of other children.

Like all children, Anthony is so much more than another statistic in this constant stream of those who are tortured and murdered. There are hundreds of photographs of him on Facebook, smiling amid his siblings and cousins.

Heather's brother David, and his wife Maria, wanted to take care of the children when they realised the level of maltreatment they were suffering, and Anthony took to calling his aunt, 'Mom'. But after one particular incident of reporting to DCFS, Heather Barron prevented them from seeing the children again.

§

Heather Barron did not have an easy childhood. But her two siblings, David and Crystal, knew the cycle of abuse could be broken, and had the presence of mind to warn their sister not to mete out the same punishments they had been subjected to as children. But instead, Heather Barron forced four of her children to kneel for hours on dry, uncooked rice, until their knees bled. Seeing no let-up, her siblings informed the Department of Children and Family Services multiple times. And her brother made a chilling prediction during one of the phone calls; that one of the children would be dead in five years if they were left in the home. It proved to be an understatement. Anthony died just three years later.

§

Heather Barron and Kareem Leiva chose a non-jury trial, which took place in the Superior Courtroom of Judge Sam Ohta during February 2023.

Reasons for non-jury (or bench) trials can include instances when a jury response is likely to be highly charged with emotion, such as in a child murder by abuse case such as this, or when a defendant may appear to have been a participant in gang activity, and is perhaps tattooed with gang identification. Another aspect is when intimidation of jurors seems likely to occur.

Kareem Leiva had admitted to investigators that he had abused the children but declared that he did not deliver the fatal blows.

Prosecuting the case were Deputy District Attorneys Saeed Teymouri and Jon Hatami, the latter having been the lead prosecutor who secured a guilty verdict in the trial of Pearl Fernandez and Isauro Aguirre, murderers of Gabriel Fernandez. They alleged that whilst Barron had abused Anthony and his siblings for many years, when Leiva appeared on the scene, the abuse soon increased.

Drs. Cho Lwin and Juan Carrillo, of the LA County Coroners Office testified about the "multiple blunt force impacts" to Anthony's brain, ranging from one day to three weeks in age, and ruled that the ten-year-old's death was a homicide, due to blunt-force head trauma. Anthony's condition was exacerbated by his starvation and dehydration, which had caused his veins to collapse.

Also testifying at the trial was Michael Gelardo, a patrol deputy at the Los Angeles County sheriff's station in Lancaster. When David and Maria Barron had attempted to keep the children safe by refusing to return them to their mother following a visit, Heather Barron reported her brother to the police.

Deputy Gelardo was sent to investigate. After speaking to the children, who told him about Leiva's abusive behaviour, he felt it was not safe to return them, and that they should stay with their uncle and aunt at that time.

In addition, Gelardo called the DCFS hotline, but told the court that he wasn't contacted by anyone following up the report. So despite the actions of this officer, and the children's concerned family, Anthony and the other children were left to their fate.

§

The brave testimony of Anthony's two younger siblings, who also suffered under Barron and Leiva's regime, was crucial to the case.

In contradiction to Leiva's denials, they described how their stepfather had dropped Anthony on his head 10 to 20 times, on the day before he died. When asked what their mother did when Anthony was lying on the carpet unable to move, the reply was: "Nothing."

It was revealed that Anthony was also smashed into the floor or furniture, burned with cigarettes, and alternately starved and force-fed.

The siblings confirmed what Anthony had told Children's Services long ago; that they were made to kneel for hours on nails or uncooked rice and to take up the position of 'The Captain's Chair'. They also told the court that punishments included being whipped all over with a belt or cord, being made to stand in a corner for hours, and being made to hold books or weights above their heads.

Heather Barron's defence attorneys claimed that Anthony's siblings were not reliable witnesses, as they had originally told deputies, during the visit to the home following the 911 call, as their brother lay dead or dying, that: "My mom doesn't hit me, nobody hits us."

The judge was sensible enough to see that this original statement was coached by the perpetrators, and that they had been made to lie about the abuse to family, police, doctors and teachers the whole of their lives. They said that their mother had warned them: "What happens in the house, stays in the house."

In court, each child was asked the difficult question of whether they loved their mother. Anthony's sister, now 13 years old, replied that she did, but that she felt a lot of other things too. His brother, now 12, said that he used to.

§

Barron's defence claimed that she was a victim of domestic violence and couldn't prevent Leiva from punishing the children. That may, or may not, be the case. But she had been abusing them for years, prior to meeting Leiva.

In an audio-tape of an interview with investigators that was played at the trial, in typical child murderer style, Barron blames Anthony for his injuries: "I promise I did not hurt my son. I did not let nobody hurt my son ... I swear he was just acting up and he threw himself because he didn't want to eat."

She also said that Anthony had told her he might be gay and that she had responded that she would "love him no matter what" because he was her "baby."

§

The judge took six days to review the evidence before proclaiming his verdict.

Heather Maxine Barron and Kareem Ernesto Leiva were found guilty on 7 March 2023, of murder in the first degree of Anthony Avalos, with the special circumstance of torture, and with the torture and abuse of two of Anthony's siblings.

**Sentencing took place on 25 April 2023, the date on which I published this book, in honour of Anthony and his family. With the death penalty off the table, they were handed down the most severe sentence possible – life imprisonment without parole.**

§

Anthony is one of the 6-7 million children in the US who are victims of alleged abuse or neglect every year, and one of around 1,800 children whose torture ends in murder.

That's 5 children, in the US alone, suffering
and dying like Anthony, every day.

Anthony will never be forgotten by his loving family. His teachers and class-mates will remember him too. And like other children who are abused to death, many of us who never knew him, hold him in our hearts and remember him in our own way. My way is by writing his story in the hope that you will read and think of the kind-hearted and friendly little boy.

Anthony loved playing football, and fishing at Apollo Park and the aqueduct at Quartz Hill. He loved Halloween, super-heroes, such as Spiderman and Batman, arts and crafts, and dancing with his siblings and cousins. Full of life, at any given moment, he would bound up to his uncle and aunties to hug them. He was protective of his young siblings and cousins, and was known for his 'knock knock' jokes.

**Anthony's Tree**, close to his Lancaster home, is a gathering place for many who remember the bright and caring little boy.

There are a number of Facebook groups in his name, including The Anthony Avalos Memorial Tree, set up by his family, in memory of the boy they loved, and Justice for Anthony Avalos. Another group, remembering Anthony, along with

Memorial Tree in Lancaster, California

Gabriel Fernandez and Noah Cuatro, is called Angels of the AV, Justice for Gabriel, Anthony and Noah.

These groups also offer a space where those who care about Anthony can find like-minded people who want to raise awareness of his story, and of other children who are **Abused To Death**.

## His name is Anthony Avalos

## Please don't forget him

# Thank You For Reading

I'm on a mission to raise awareness of child murder by abuse, and this is my sixth published book about children who have been Abused To Death.

I began writing when I discovered that this horrific crime had happened within the family of a friend, and I couldn't eat or sleep when I discovered the numbers of children being murdered, and the extent of their suffering.

> If you have been moved by Anthony's story, please give this book an Amazon **star rating or review.**

I love hearing from my readers, so if you wish to contact me, you are most welcome to do so on:
**jessicajackson@jesstruecrime.com**

## Help To Protect Children Like Anthony

Please just review in your usual way, or the QR code or link should help you to get back to the book's page:

mybook.to/AnthonyAvalos

Then scroll **waaay down**
until you see **Write a Review**
(usually on the left side)

Reviews help to spread the word about abuse and I appreciate every single one. Just a star rating or a few words is enough.

# Your Next Book in the Series

*You can see my full series after a few more pages, but if you've read them all (thank you), here's a preview of the next child whose story I'm writing.*

On New Year's Day 2018, emergency services were called to a mobile home in Wayne County, Michigan, where a little girl lay unresponsive on the bathroom floor.

 Four year old Gabrielle Barrett's mother claimed that while she was busy making pancakes at the stove, her daughter had run herself a hot bath, and stepped into the scalding water, causing her fatal injuries.

But in truth, Gabrielle had been tortured and abused for weeks, culminating in her horrific death on the day when most of us were celebrating the start of a new year.

Loved by other family members, Gabby also found a safe haven at school. But no one was able to save the little girl from the torture inflicted by her drug-addicted mother and sadistic boyfriend.

Join my Readers' List, Follow Me on Amazon, and Follow Me on Facebook, to be the first to know when Gabby's story will be available on Amazon.

# Join Us On Facebook

Want to connect with me and join a community of people who want to prevent child abuse?

I honour the murdered children on my Facebook page, and if you'd like to come and say 'Hi' on one of my posts, it'd be great to see you there.

**By mistake, Facebook recently deleted my Page, and I lost all my loyal Followers, posts and comments.**

I'd love you to **Follow Me:**

Just scan this code:

Or use this link:

**Jessica Jackson Author**

Or within Facebook, type into the search bar:

**Jessica Jackson Author**

## An Invitation

Would you like to **join my Readers' List**, by picking up your free ebook overleaf?

*And would you please do me a great favour?*

Because my books are so sad, I double-check that you want to join my Readers' List, and so you'll receive a quick email from me, to ask you to **confirm your place**.

> *Can you please reply either **Yes or No** to this email? It only takes a few seconds but is **incredibly** helpful to me.*

**If you don't receive the email almost instantly, please check Junk/Spam – I can't add you without your reply.**

*Thank you; I really appreciate this.*

# Readers' List Benefits

Members get special offers, along with each new release at the subscriber price. And if you'd like to be more involved, you can **suggest children to include**, give your input on cover design, and lots more.

> *I'm always interested in what my readers think, and so on the day after you've confirmed your place and joined us, I'll email you with the question:*
>
> *"ARE THEY MONSTERS?"*
>
> *I'd love to include your opinion in my readers' poll, and invite you to enter the draw for a free signed book and personalised bookmark.*

So, get your free ebook overleaf, and thank you in advance if you decide to join us.

# Pick Up Your Free Ebook and Join Us!

Isaiah Torres was just six years old when he was abused to death in the most appalling way.

*Pick up your copy of your free ebook*

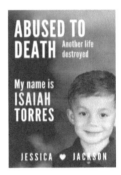     **Just scan this code:**

**Or use this link:**

https://BookHip.com/VNGMZJJ

*Then be sure to click Yes or No on the quick email I'll send to confirm your place – it looks like this:*

Yes thanks, I'd love to join, Jess

OR

No, I won't join just now, Jess

# Find All My Books on Amazon

**Find them in your usual way, or you can ...**

Search Amazon for:

**Abused To Death by Jessica Jackson**

**Or scan this code:**

**Or use this link:**

viewbook.at/abused-series

Then choose your book.

If you wish, you can also **Follow** Me on Amazon.

# Don't Miss A Thing

**Pick up your free ebook:**

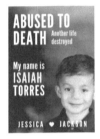

**Just scan this code:**

https://BookHip.com/VNGMZJJ

**And reply to your Yes or No email**

**Follow me on Facebook:**

Jessica Jackson Author

**Follow me on Amazon:**

author.to/jessicajackson

*(Ensure your Settings in **Communications / Preferences in Amazon** are set to receive info about new releases.)*

# Prevention

Abuse and murder occur for complex reasons, and prevention is an immense task. These are my own views on how we can move towards prevention of this horrendous crime, echoing those of the World Health Organisation (WHO).

1 - End physical discipline of children
2 - Regulate homeschooling effectively
3 - An outlet for caregivers' anger
4 - Listen to the children when they report abuse
5 - Improve communication between agencies
6 - Safe places for unwanted babies
7 - Educate the parents of the future:
  - that a baby communicates by crying
  - how to give love, safety and guidance
  - about bladder & bowel habits of children

# Warning Signs of Abuse

There are various factors that might suggest a child is being abused. This list has been compiled by the NSPCC, but is not exhaustive:
- unexplained changes in behaviour or personality
- becoming withdrawn or anxious
- becoming uncharacteristically aggressive
- lacking social skills and having few friends
- poor bonding or relationship with a parent
- knowledge of issues inappropriate for their age
- running away or going missing
- wearing clothes which cover their body

### *And I would add:*

- marks and bruises on the body
- being secretive
- stealing (often food)
- weight loss
- inappropriate clothing
- poor hygiene / unkempt
- tiredness
- inability to concentrate
- being overly eager to please the adult
- the child *telling* you that they're being hurt
  (alarmingly, this is often ignored)
- a non-verbal child *showing* you that they're being hurt

- the adult removing the child from school after they have come under suspicion

*And when faced with an adult who you suspect of abusing a child, don't unquestioningly accept what they say, but instead:*

A - Assume nothing

B - Be vigilant

C - Check everything

D - Do something

*Listen to the children and report what you see*

## TO REPORT CHILD ABUSE IN THE USA & CANADA

The National Child Abuse Hotline:1-800-422-4453

If a child is in immediate danger, call 911


## TO REPORT CHILD ABUSE IN THE UK

Adults, call the NSPCC on 0808 800 5000

Children, call Childline on 0800 1111

Or if there is risk of imminent danger, ring 999


## TO REPORT CHILD ABUSE IN AUSTRALIA

The National Child Abuse Reportline: 131-478

Children, call: 1800-55-1800

If a child is in immediate danger, call 000

## Selected Resources

- Boy's mother heard telling investigators she didn't hurt him, Lisa Bartley, ABC7.com, 01 February 2023

- City News Service, Antelope Valley Times, 27 January 2023

- Khaleda Rahman, 'Who Is Heather Barron?' newsweek.com 8 March 2023

- The horrific death of Anthony Avalos and the many missed chances to save him – Garrett Therolf, LA Times, 4 September 2019

*Disclaimer*

My aim is to tell stories of murdered children with a combination of accuracy and readability, to heighten awareness of child torture and murder, and to explore ways of preventing further tragedies. I have relied on the factual information available to me during my research, and where I have added characters or dramatised events to better tell the child's story, I believe I have done so without significantly altering the important details. If anyone has further information about the children, particularly if you knew them and have anecdotes to share about their life, I would be delighted to hear from you. Likewise, whilst every attempt has been made to make contact with copyright holders, if I have unwittingly used any material when I was not at liberty to do so, please contact me so that this can be rectified at:

jessicajackson@jesstruecrime.com